Kendall's Kindness
BY: CHERIE DORTCH- WALDEN

Written for Kendall Aubrey Walden,
By Cherie Dortch-Walden

Being kind is cool.

Kindness means being friendly, loving, giving and mostly being careful not to cause any hurt to others.

When we are kind to someone, it makes them feel good. It also makes us feel good. It even makes those watching us be kind, feel good too.

That means, kindness can be contagious!

Being kind gives us better
health too.

Engaging in acts of kindness produces hormones called endorphins. My *Gigi* says these are natural painkillers.

My gigi is a mental health therapist. A therapist is someone you talk to in confidence, who helps you work out your problems and learn healthy ways to cope in life.

Sometimes when we don't feel good inside,
we're not kind.
That's when we need kindness the most.

When we don't feel good inside, we should let our parents know so that they can help us or find us a therapist, like my Gigi.

We should always be kind.

Kindness increases your happiness.

Being kind means showing empathy for others, or try to understand how someone else is feeling. We pay attention and try to understand someone else's experience or emotions.

We self-reflect to make sure we are using kind words, and simply being kind.
- Thank you
- Appologies
- May I ...
- Respected
- Sorry

When we self-reflect, we
can think before we speak,
or act.

Some of us have different skin color, different hair color, and even different eye color, but we can still be kind to one another and know that we are all uniquely created.

Kindness is expressing appreciation to the nice lady who holds the door open for you.

Kindness is reading a book to your little sister. My big sister Nirvana reads to me.

Kindness is also paying attention while
your sister is being kind enough to read to
you.

Kindness is helping your mom clean the house.

Kindness is telling your daddy how handsome he is.

Kindness is giving lot's of hugs and kisses
to my grandma and my gigi.

And more hugs to my grandpa and poppa.

And do all of these things without expecting anything in return.

Most of all, kindness is telling yourself
how beautiful and how awesome you are!

Being kind to yourself is most important. It
makes it easier for you to be kind to others.

Being aligned with feelings of happiness is
kindness toward yourself.

VOCABULARY WORDS

ALIGNED- TO BE IN LINE WITH SOMETHING OR IN AGREEMENT WITH.

APPRECIATION-A FEELING OF THANKS.

CONSIDERATE- THOUGHTFUL OF THE FEELINGS OF OTHERS.

COPE- TO DEAL WITH PROBLEMS AND OVERCOME THEM.

EMOTIONS- A PERSON'S INNER FEELINGS.

EMPATHY- UNDERSTANDING HOW SOMEONE ELSE IS FEELING.

EXPRESSING- TO SHOW OR TELL YOUR THOUGHTS OR FEELINGS.

GENEROUS- BEING HAPPY TO GIVE.

KINDNESS- THE QUALITY OF BEING FRIENDLY, GENEROUS AND CONSIDERATE. A KIND ACT.

SELF-REFLECT- BEING ABLE TO SEE AND THINK ABOUT YOUR OWN BEHAVIOR, THOUGHTS AND FEELINGS

THERAPIST- ONE WHO HELPS YOU UNDERSTAND YOURSELF BETTER AND HELPS YOU WITH SOLVING SOCIAL, EMOTIONAL AND PSYCHOLOGICAL PROBLEMS.

THOUGHTFUL- GIVING CAREFUL ATTENTION TO OTHER'S NEEDS.

TRANSFERENCE- WHEN SOMEONE REDIRECTS THEIR EMOTIONS AND FEELINGS ABOUT ONE PERSON ONTO SOMEONE ELSE.

UNIQUE- BEING THE ONLY ONE OF ITS KIND.